Cosmic Travels of Sirius and Staila

From the Alps to the Moon

by

Jitka & Václav Ourednik

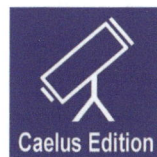

Caelus Edition

www.caelus.club

Cosmic Travels of Sirius and Staila – From the Alps to the Moon
Translated from German by Václav Ourednik
Copyright © Caelus Edition
ISBN:978-0-9863486-0-0 Hardcover 2015
ISBN: 978-0-9863486-2-4 Softcover 2016

Les Voyages Cosmiques de Sirius et Staila - Des Alpes à la Lune
Translated from English by Matilde Bingemer and Ida Friedmann
Copyright © Caelus Edition 2015
ISBN: 978-0-9863486-3-1   Softcover

Vesmírné výpravy Síria a Staily – Z alpských velehor na Měsíc
Czech original
Copyright © Caelus Edition 2014, 2015
ISBN: 978-0-9863486-1-7   Softcover

Die Weltraum-Reisen von Sirius und Staila – Von der Val Müstair zum Mond
German original
Copyright © Südostschweiz Buchverlag 2013
ISBN: 978-3-90-60-64   Hardcover

Cover and artwork: © Jitka Ourednik

www.caelus.club

To our grown-up son Ondřej
and to all children – young and old -
for whom their kin often don't find enough time.

CONTENTS

The authors released a radioplay of this book in April 2016.
A copy of it on CD can be obtained at *www.caelus.club* .

The Valley of Müstair (Val Müstair)

ACKNOWLEDGEMENT

We would like to thank Olga Kukal
- our dear friend and Jitka's companion during a beautifully adventurous childhood -
for her valuable comments and review of the manuscript.

We also thank Jarmila Kašparová for her assistance with illustrations.

Village Lü

E las stailas vi dal tschêl
Dischan quant cha´l muond ais bel.

Our skies full of shimmering lights
share the world's beautiful sights.

From the Romansh poem *Saira* by Chatrina Filli (1914-1983)

AND THEY STILL DO EXIST, THE TRUE FAIRY TALES !

They say today's children don't like fairy tales anymore. Fairy tales are just for mom and dad. But who can blame kids for lacking interest, when new discoveries and modern technologies are found everywhere at their very finger tips -- on TV or just a mouse click away. But, be sure of it, one thing continuing to thrill kids nowadays are exciting stories that seem fantastic, but still reveal the truth. It is this kind of story that you will find in our book series of which this is the first volume. We will dive into the depths of the cosmos and meet dragons, witches, mighty gods, and discover fabulous kingdoms. We will fly by red giants and white dwarfs and visit places where time stands still. But most amazingly, all you'll read here describes the real universe that surrounds us. So come, join us, and see for yourself.

1

The colors of the Moon

2

CHAPTER 1:
AN OBSERVATORY IN THE ALPS AND TWO FOUR-LEGGED FRIENDS

High in the towering Alps in the eastern corner of Switzerland, in the canton Graubünden, is nestled a tiny, sunny village named Lü. Surrounded by enchanting nature, it looks down into a picturesque valley, the Val Müstair.

Staila and Sírius

People come to this area from near and far to find peace and pristine nature, and to watch and photograph rare animals and plants. But they also find something else that is becoming increasingly rare in our world – a dark and transparent night sky displaying thousands of sparkling stars. It is this type of night sky that lets us look deep into the cosmos. Therefore, at the end of 2009,

the International Year of Astronomy, a new astronomical observatory was built in Lü. It was built for all who love the stars, and also for those who adore nature in the mountains. The observatory's name is *Lü-Stailas*, meaning *Light of Stars* in the Romansh language of the locals.

Big Dog constellation

The observatory was built by two scientists, Jitka and Václav. They moved here from a large city and live now amidst this beautiful alpine nature together with their two four-legged friends, the dachshund Sirius and his friend, the black cat Staila. At night, Jitka and Václav observe and take photographs of the deep sky, and they write articles and also books, like this one.

Sirius is the older of the two and he loves drawing and reading, especially about nature, astronomy, and also about old tales and legends. He is great friends with the young and always very curious Staila. Although she teases her companion quite often, she actually admires him and likes to hear his interesting tales and explanations.

The names of the four-legged friends are by no means accidental. Sirius is the brightest star in our sky. You can find it in the constellation Big Dog. According to an old tale, the dog Sirius and his beloved master – the hunter Orion – were both lifted into the skies by gods to shine forever as a symbol of true loyalty. And the little cat Staila, black as the night above the Val Müstair, sports a tuft of white fur on her chest resembling a star. When he wants to be especially gentle, the doggie calls her Starlet.

One day, the sun was setting behind the Alpine ridges and the white head of the Ortler was bathed in red from the afterglow. Finally, the ancient mountain giant found its well-deserved sleep. The little golden branches of the larch trees were swinging gently in the soft breeze and the air was filled with a wonderful odor. Ahhhhhh, what an enchanting autumn evening! The sky turned darker and darker and the full Moon began to cover the landscape in its cold light. Staila and Sirius were overwhelmed by this beautiful display of nature. They stopped playing and sat quietly, side by side, gazing up.

Fortunately, their alpine village was spared from the dazzling lights of street lamps and ad panels of modern cities. It is because of the latter that, sadly, the grandiose spectacle of a starry night nowadays remains out of reach for most people. Light pollution is steadily encroaching on our planet and becomes harmful in many ways to humans and other animals. It deprives us of sleep and makes hunting for nocturnal creatures difficult. The artificial light disturbs insects and birds during their migration so they lose their way and perish. Even from space one can nowadays see the Earth illuminated by industrial city lights, with truly dark areas being drowned out by artificial light.

Therefore, today's astronomers have to move their telescopes to remote and isolated places like high mountain peaks, deserts, or lonely islands. Only there can they escape the reach of glaring city lights – the ever-expanding sources of light pollution. And here they also find, apart from pristine skies, the best weather conditions for exploration of the universe: a dry climate, wide-open views, and a stable and clear atmosphere.

City   Outskirts   Countryside   Best sky

Light polution

For many years, Jitka and Václav searched for the best possible place in central Europe to set up their observatory. They found it high in the Alps, on the slopes of the beautiful Val Müstair. Here, in the easternmost corner of Switzerland at almost 2000 meters above sea level, one is far away from large cities and mighty mountain ridges hold back rain and cloudy weather. At night, one sees almost as many stars as one can find in desert regions or on lonely islands.

The two friends were gazing at the starlit sky.

"Sirius", started the little cat suddenly, "do you know who placed these beautiful stars up there in the sky and what keeps them from falling down to us?"

"But Staila", replied her friend in a friendly voice. He liked it when his playmate asked him questions, so he could demonstrate his knowledge. "Nobody just 'put them up' there. The stars are gigantic suns floating in space. They formed a long, long time ago, and since they are so far from us, we see them in the sky just as tiny sparkling specks of light."

"So all we can see in the night sky is the universe? I heard it is infinite", wondered Staila.

"Yes, it is immense", said Sirius, "and what we can see from Earth is just a tiny part of it. In the universe, there are innumerable stars and some are a hundred or thousand times bigger than our Sun. And like the Sun, most of these stars have planets orbiting them and many of the planets are orbited by their moons. Stars, planets, and moons form *planetary systems*, and thousands of millions, or billions, of stars and planetary systems form a *galaxy* and

circle around its center. The universe is thus composed of billions of galaxies..."

"Wait, Sirius, not so fast", the kitty complained, "you are losing me. So that means that our solar system with the Earth is part of some galaxy?"

"Wait just a second. Better, I will draw this for you", said Sirius who loves to draw while he explains. After briefly disappearing into the house, he came back with a notepad and colored pens and drew for Staila spheres, circles, and spirals.

Staila with drawing by Sirius

Milky way with Ortler

"Of course, I cannot draw all the galaxies – the paper is much too small. The Earth together with the other planets…"

Staila interrupted her friend again: "Actually, what's the difference between a star and a planet?"

"A star, like our Sun, shines and produces tremendous heat by itself. A planet doesn't do that. On the other hand, it is illuminated by the Sun and so becomes visible in the night sky."

Staila nodded and Sirius continued: "OK, so our solar system belongs to a galaxy that we call the *Milky Way*. Here, in the Val Müstair, we can easily see it in the sky with the naked eye. Of course not tonight, the full Moon is much too bright and outshines all but the brightest stars.

But look, I have a photograph of the Milky Way above the Ortler on a moonless night."

Sirius took the picture and pointed out the bright band over the mountain ridge with his paw. "This is our galaxy. People call it the Milky Way, because, with some imagination, it looks like milk spilled across the sky. In reality, our galaxy is a disc made of stars, gas, and dust, floating through space like an island. Our solar system is located about two thirds of the distance between the galactic center and the outer edge."

The cat examined the photograph carefully and asked: "Sirius, tell me, all those stars that we can see from the Earth, do they all belong to our Milky Way?"

"Yes, Starlet", nodded Sirius, "that's right. But from a dark area like the Val Müstair we can see by naked eye yet another galaxy. It is very distant and, even without moonlight, appears as only a very faint and gray little speck in the sky. Look here, I also brought you its picture. It is the great *Andromeda Galaxy* in the constellation *Androme*da.

Andromeda Galaxy

Perseus liberating Andromeda

Vaclav often shows this galaxy to visitors of Lü-Stailas and took this photograph through a telescope.

Since Staila admired with great interest the picture held up to her, Sirius continued: "This spiral galaxy is named Andromeda after a lovely girl from an ancient legend. According to Greek mythology, the poor girl, daughter of king Cepheus and queen Cassiopeia, was chained to a rock as sacrifice to a terrible sea monster by the people to save their city from destruction. Fortunately, the brave hero Perseus arrived in time on his winged horse Pegasus and saved the desperate princess from the grips of the monster."

Sirius continued: "To look deeper into the universe and to take pictures like this, we need a telescope."

With great interest, Staila looked at both photographs. "So, how far are the stars that we can see by naked eye and how far can we see through a telescope?"

The little dachshund plunged into deep thought. "Many visitors often ask this question.

The speed of light

10

The farthest star in our galaxy visible by naked eye is about 4,000 light years away. Our neighbor galaxy, Andromeda, is visible from a distance of about 2.5 million light years. With a telescope, however, we can see stars and other objects that are even billions of light years distant and …."

"Wait, wait, Sirius!" interrupted Staila impatiently, "what is actually a *light year*?"

Again, Sirius reached with his paw for pen and paper. "OK, I'll give you an example. Imagine a city one hour by car away from us and the car drives with a speed of 80 km/hr. How far is the city?"

Staila looked at the picture and thought aloud: "Could it be that...? Ah, nonsense….now I got it! The city is 80 km away from us."

"Excellent! And now, tell me how far the Moon is when it takes the light about one second to reach it?"

"But what is the speed of light?" Staila asked cleverly.

Sirius turned over the paper and made a new drawing: "Nothing is faster than light. In one second – or before you can say *twenty-one* – it travels 300,000 kilometers. If a rocket could fly that fast, in one second it could circle the Earth seven times."

Staila quickly made a mental calculation: "So, you say, the Moon is about one light second away from us. That means its distance is about 300,000 kilometers."

"Well done, Staila!" Sirius praised his little friend. "And do you know how far away the Sun is? It takes its rays of light eight and a half minutes to reach us, so the distance of the Sun is 8.5 light minutes….In that time, you could drink a couple of bowls of milk and I could eat a big sausage without breaking a sweat," murmured Sirius and started to lick his lips at the last thought.

"And it takes light much longer still to get to us from the center of the Milky Way. Imagine, Staila, it has been on its way for about 30,000 years!"

"But why do they measure distances in space with the speed of light?" asked Staila shaking her head.

"Well, because it is easier for astronomers to measure such immense distances in light years, rather than in miles or kilometers. Otherwise, they would have to cope with terribly long numbers. Just one light year is 9,460,528,400,000 kilometers. It's already tough to read this number: 9 trilion, 460 billion, 528 million, and 400 thousand..."

"Oh boy, Sirius, my head is spinning from all these big numbers and distances," complained the cat.

Seven times around the Earth

"But Starlet," the dachshund started calming down his friend, "the size of the Milky Way is nothing compared to the immense dimensions of the universe. The distances to other galaxies are measured in millions, even billions of light years. That means, their light, which we see now, had to start its journey millions and billions of years ago. Do you understand? Each time we are looking up into the sky, we see a picture of its past: we see the history of the universe!"

Staila jumped up and became all excited. "But Sirius! This means that the light reaching us from the stars we are seeing can be much older than our Earth and the entire solar system!" She was proud to know that the age of the Earth is a 'mere' 4.5 billion years.

"Yes," gasped Sirius now also quivering with excitement. This was exactly what had just crossed his mind as well. He continued to think aloud: "But this must also be true the other way around. If somebody, or something, is watching the Earth from another planet four thousand light years away, he doesn't see us but instead is watching pharaohs building the pyramids."

Dreaming of the cosmos

"And the extinct dinosaurs, that roamed the Earth in prehistoric times, would be visible to beings on planets over 60 million light years away!" miaowed the cat as her tail trembled with excitement.

Sirius and Staila started imagining how distant other worlds would have to be for their inhabitants to follow the history of our planet: the birth of the Earth, the appearance of first life, long extinct animals and plants, the Ice Ages, and the lives of prehistoric hunters. Slowly, the eyelids of both our friends became heavy from all the thinking. In their plush igloos, they soon rolled up into two fluffy fur balls and sank deeper and deeper into their dreams of the endless cosmos strewn with planets, stars, and galaxies far, far away. They saw strange worlds and kingdoms where small beings like themselves, or completely different creatures, looked up in the direction of the Earth. And yet, they saw neither a Staila nor a Sirius , s nc e both of their images had first to travel thousands or millions of years in order to reach these distant, alien worlds... .

CHAPTER 2:
THE MIRACULOUS TELESCOPE

Did you hear that? The wind was whistling through the tree branches and suddenly there emerged strange squeaking and beating noises. Cat and doggie, both sleepy, rubbed their eyes. Somebody was on the terrace! Sirius growled in a dark voice and bravely made a round of the premises. After a while, Staila heard his muffled voice: "There is nobody, Staila. It's just the wind playing with the door of the dome."

Staila approached her friend slowly on her silent cat paws: "Let's peek inside, Sirius," she whispered mischievously into his ear.

"Oh my goodness, Staila! You gave me a good scare." yelped Sirius and took a deep breath.

"Don't be angry, Sirius. Each time, when I see people viewing stars at night, I always have a big urge to ask them if they would also let me look at the universe through the telescope."

Has it ever crossed your minds that animals also have secret wishes? Sirius knew that he shouldn't do such a thing without permission. But looking at his begging friend he said: "OK, OK, this one time. Let's have a look inside. But be careful not to knock down the computer or to get tangled in the cables."

Swiftly, both friends slipped through the open door into the dome. "See this metal pier? That firmly supports the telescope," Sirius pointed with his paw to the structure at the dome's center. "With it, you can look into every corner of the universe and discover and take pictures of unknown and fantastic things."

But what was this buzzing and humming noise? Both friends cocked their ears. Suddenly, they heard a deep and soft voice: "Welcome! I didn't even notice that somebody was knocking. You both seem to be interested in stargazing. I can certainly help you."

Sirius and Staila cringed and huddled closer together. "Who…who's there? Who's talking?"

"Now, now. You are looking straight at me…!"

"Oh my goodness! The telescope – it speaks…!" Doubtfully, the cat looked at her friend. The latter shook his head and started to sniff nervously around the dome's interior.

A new friend

"Well, if you animals can speak – why not me? I am the Robotic Telescope and I know that I can do a lot of things. And if I happen to lack knowledge of something, I can easily find it in my computer or on the internet. I can look far into the depths of the universe and take pictures of everything I like."

"Good gracious! Staila, the telescope is really speaking to us!" the dog uttered with excitement. Immediately, however, he remembered how impolite it is to speak about somebody as if he was not present, or fo r that matter to enter a room without knocking and greeting.

"Good evening, dear Telescope. My name is Sirius and this is my friend Staila. We apologize for having intruded without permission. We live here at the observatory, and our long-time wish has always been to visit you."

The Teleskop about itself

The Telescope was evidently pleased. "But I know you very well. You are the ones running around the place and peeking inside now and then when I have guests - always thought I would love to chat with you sometime. It will be a great pleasure to spend one of my miraculous nights with you two. But first, and I hope you don't mind, I'd like to ask you something."

Staila and Sirius nodded eagerly. They felt a fabulous adventure was awaiting them.

"The night sky has always stirred up a lot of curiosity in humans. But do you two know when people used a telescope to look into space for the first time?"

Sirius, who loves to read books and

magazines about astronomy, knew immediately: "I think the first telescope was built a few centuries ago. But it was much smaller and simpler than you, Sir."

The Telescope nodded and added: "Yes, you are correct. The first telescope was built at the beginning of the 17th century. It had two *glass lenses* but no mirrors like I have today. The lenses were mounted on both ends of a narrow metal *tube* with the *objective end* looking towards the sky and gathering light and the *visual end* where you can look through the *eyepiece*. That telescope was very simple and magnified just 3 times. On the shelf above you is a book showing a picture of this first telescope compared to a modern one like myself."

The Telescope took a breath and continued: "If we look into space, of course, we want to see as far as possible and as many details as possible. It is obvious: the brighter and bigger a galaxy, the more we can see. Therefore, preferably, a well-designed instrument like myself', the Telescope's pride was evident, "holds a large objective in a correspondingly wider tube. With a larger aperture, more light is gathered and funneled to the eye through the eyepiece, which results in a brighter image. I even have groups of lenses installed in front of and behind my large mirror that help me to produce very sharp and detailed images of any object magnified up to 600 times."

Sirius and Staila listened attentively, their eyes looking up in awe at the talking Telescope.

"While in earlier times, exploring the night skies was only for professional astronomers, nowadays anybody can enjoy stargazing with a telescope. Do you see the big red box under my tube? This is my *mount* – my brain – always connected with these cables to the computer. All the programs and data stored in its memory allow me to find thousands of stars and other deep sky objects. Like this, I can get commands and requests either directly here in the dome or from anywhere over the internet – even from the other side of the Earth."

Meanwhile, Sirius and Staila were completely aglow with enthusiasm. In unison, they almost implored the Telescope: "Oh please, please, can we look at something in the sky tonight?"

The Telescope was evidently flattered with the friends' great interest and their wish to observe. Like all who love their work, it was thrilled to talk about it. The electronic humming and buzzing filling the room increased and without further delay a broad opening in the dome offered a view of the night sky.

"Just come closer and let me know what you would like to see."

Kitty and doggie turned their heads towards the dome opening. Their eyes fell immediately on the silvery full Moon.

CHAPTER 3:
WHERE DOES MOONLIGHT COME FROM ?

"The moonlight has some sort of a cooling beauty to it", said Sirius in a dreamy mood.

"Yes, tonight I'd see every mouse running by", the cat agreed in a more practical way.

"But that counts for the mouse as well and it would have no problems to stay out of reach of your sharp little claws", laughed Sirius. "O yes, during full Moon it's not the best time for us nocturnal hunters," he sighed.

"Do you see all the shadows out there in the moonlight?" Staila whispered and quickly closed the door of the dome, with her hackles up. "They say the full Moon has magical forces. It seems to help sorcery. During full Moon, witches would ride on their brooms and at its sight, man or beast can turn into bloodthirsty werewolves…"

While the Telescope chuckled with amusement, the little dachshund remained serious. "I don't believe in werewolves and witches. But I must admit that we dogs have a weakness for the full Moon. In its silvery shine, we are always overwhelmed with such a wonderful nostalgia. Turning our noses towards the Moon we then link with all the dogs and wolves in the world with a long and passionate howling so that all can witness this magic moment. But where this deep longing peppered with sadness comes from, nobody knows."

Staila fell into deep thought. "But, actually, how come the Moon is shining?"

"That's just a saying. The Moon doesn't shine itself like some lantern or a candle". Sirius looked at his friend underneath his eyebrows. "It gets its light from the Sun and here on Earth we see a reflected portion of that light."

"But the Sun set a long time ago", replied Staila.

"True, it set for us here in the Val Müstair, but for others it is noon or the Sun is just rising. You know that the Earth is round and turns on its axis in front of the Sun…"

"Axis?", wondered the little cat.

Since Sirius hesitated with his explanation, the Telescope tried to help out.

A mysterious full Moon

"The Earth's axis is like a thin rod going straight through the center of our planet, around which it spins like a gigantic ball. Depending on which side of the Earth is facing the Sun there is day on one half of the planet and night on the other. But the Moon, also illuminated by the Sun, is far above us in the sky so that we still see it lit by sunshine even when we down here are already in the dark."

"Aha", nodded Staila and continued the thought. "It is the same as here in the mountains. While the valley floor is already in shadow, people down there see that high above them – like here in Lü - the Sun still shines for many hours."

CHAPTER 4:
THE MYSTERIOUS MAN–IN–THE–MOON

Meanwhile, the pale Moon had climbed up high in the sky and the observatory was filled with a heart-warming atmosphere full of camaraderie and curiosity.

"Did you ever notice, my friends", the Telescope said with a humming undertone, "how the face of the Moon is constantly changing? Once, it is a round silver disc then again a thin crescent open to the right or left. And there are nights during which the Moon is invisible."

Staila sat up straight, while tightening her tail around her forepaws. "But of course – everybody knows about that for sure!", she said. "But I have to admit, I don't know the reason for it. Just heard some tales and legends talking about it. One talks about an Indian sorceress weaving a basket around the Moon. Her aim is to bring the Moon down to Earth and make it shine just for her. Day after day the basket walls grow higher and higher while the Moon gradually disappears into the dark. However, the enchantress does not realize to what extent her selfish intent has made the Indian gods angry. That is to say, they decided to destroy the world the very

first night after her completion of the basket. It is therefore very fortunate that this sorceress is watched by a vigilant dog who knows the Moon has to shine for everybody. Whenever the woman finishes her weaving, this brave guardian jumps up and starts to tear the basket apart, gradually freeing the Moon from its imprisonment, and the enchantress has to start her labor over and over again."

"Nice explanation – but as you say, it's just a legend", said the Telescope. "Can one of you tell me the real reason for the changes in the Moon's face?" Its inviting, one-eyed stare went to the two four-legged friends, sweeping from one to the other.

Sirius winked at Staila, but after she remained silent as a snowflake in the night, he took up the challenge: "I have often read about this. The Moon circles the Earth as her constant companion – *a natural satellite*…"

"What does that mean, *a natural satellite*?" Staila interrupted abruptly.

"A natural satellite is a celestial body circling around its planet", explained the

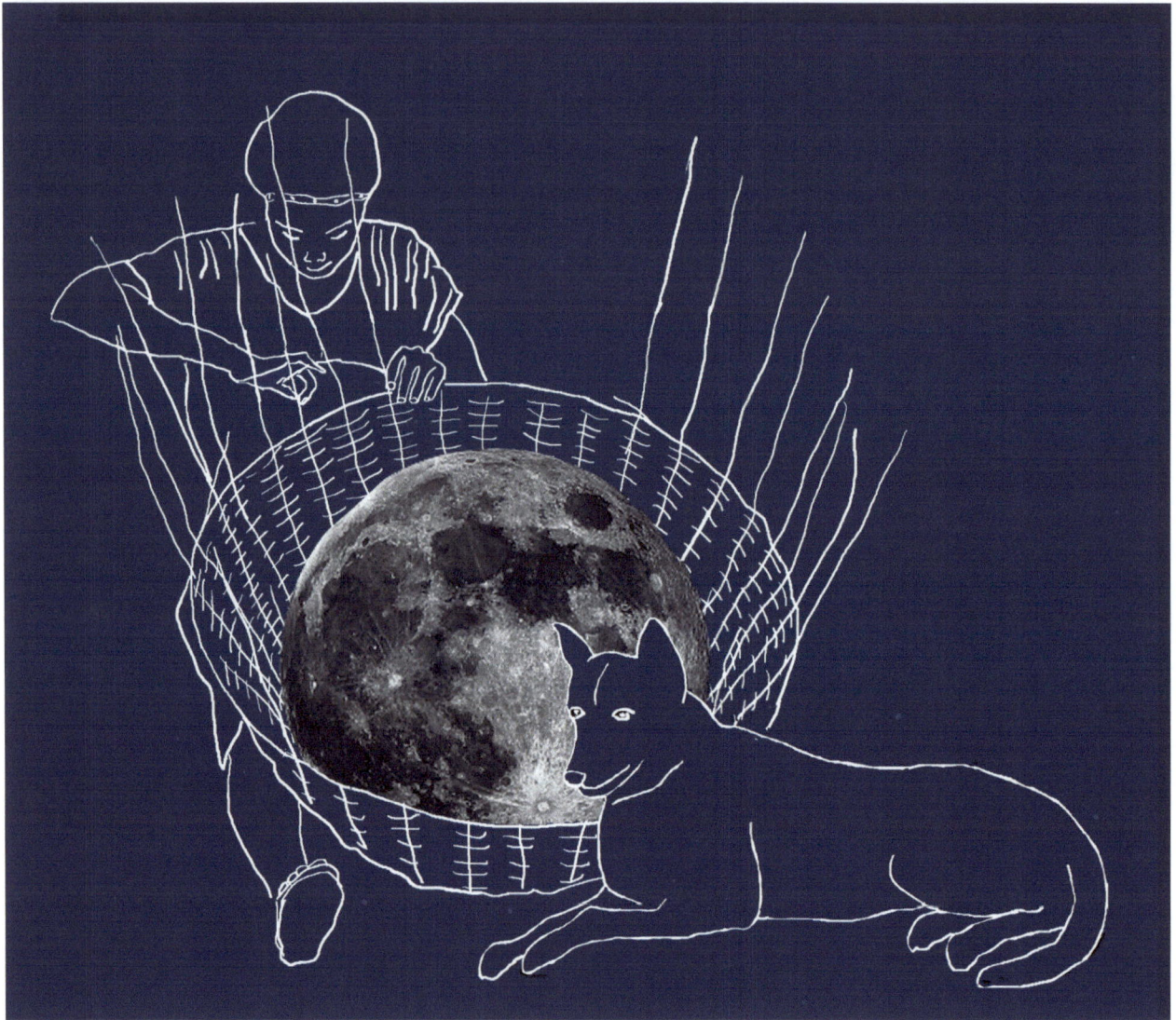

The Indian tale

dog readily. "We also call it a moon. The Earth has just one moon but other planets in the solar system have many – or none." Before Sirius could go on, Staila interrupted again: "Are there also 'unnatural' satellites…?"

Sirius gave it a brief thought and replied: "Sure, but these we call *artificial satellites*. They do not come from space but are man-made and have been shot into orbit around the Earth. The first such satellite named *Sputnik* was sent into space by the Russians in 1957. One year later, the Americans followed with *Explorer*. Today, there are thousands of man-made satellites up there. They are important tools for exploring the Earth and space but also crucial for the weather forecasts, communication, traffic monitoring, and the TV. And not to forget – the military uses satellites to monitor human activities."

Impatiently, Sirius wagged his tail. "OK, so, as we said, the Moon is a natural satellite of the Earth. When we look from the north, it orbits the planet in the same direction as the Earth's rotation, namely, counterclockwise. One orbit takes 29.5 days."

"And does the Moon also turn, or rotate, around its own axis, like the Earth?", Staila asked again full of curiosity.

"Yes, but much slower. While the Earth's rotation takes 24 hours, the Moon needs 29.5 days. One day on the Moon is therefore exactly as long as its orbit around the Earth."

The little cat nodded eagerly and came closer to the others. Sirius continued with his explanations: "This is the reason why we always see the same side of the Moon – never the other. Earth and Moon are both locked in their mutual gravitational grip and attract each other, while the planet allows the Moon to show but one side. The latter, on the other hand, sets the Earth's oceans into motion when it hovers above them. That way, it creates the high and low tides that are so important to life on our planet."

Sirius returned to his pens and paper and started drawing. "But let's get back to the changing face of the Moon. It's created by the motion of the satellite around the Earth and its position in space in relation to the Sun and the observer – and not, as many may think, by the shadow of the Earth. Look, I can show it to you in the next two pictures.

The first picture shows the Earth, the Moon, and the Sun as we would see them from space. The sunlight is coming from the right, and here to the left I drew the Earth. To show Moon's orbit around it, I drew the satellite several times and linked each position with arrows to show the movement: once between Sun and Earth, then above the latter, then here on the left, and then again beneath it. The part of the Moon that is turned away from the Sun is in the shadow and so it is dark.

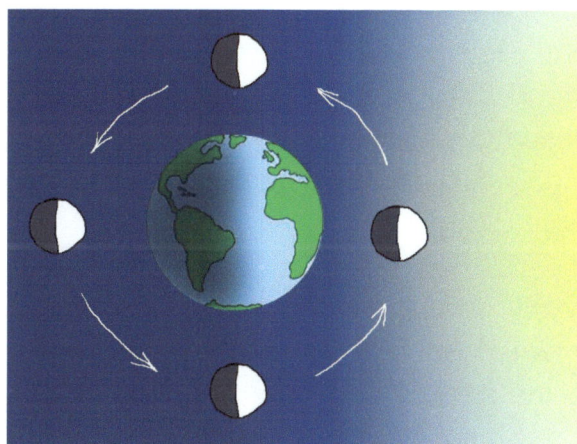

Looking from space

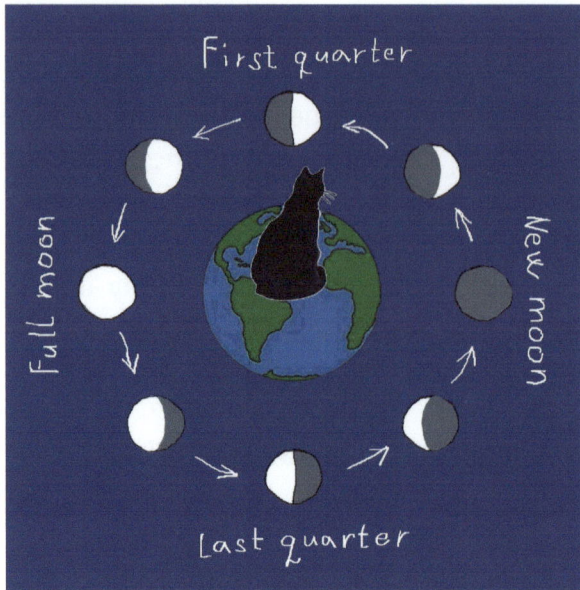

Lunation from Earth

This second picture will demonstrate how the Moon appears to us here on Earth. To show this I'll draw you, Staila, sitting here and observing the repeating change of the lunar shape. This cycle of changes we call the *Moon phases* or the *lunation*."

The dog smiled and drew his black friend sitting on the Earth. "Now, let's assume you look at the sky when the Moon is just between you and the Sun…"

"Wait", Staila cut off her friend again and frowned while Sirius drew a small circle to the right of the Earth, "but that means the Moon is up during daylight. And since the side that I am seeing is not even illuminated – I think I don't see the Moon at all?

"Right, you don't," agreed the dog, delighted that his friend was such a smart cookie.

At this point, the so far silent Telescope took up the conversation: "For your information, this phase is called *new Moon*, because it starts a new *Moon cycle*, or *lunation*."

Sirius filled his circle with black to symbolize the new Moon, which neither Staila nor anybody else could see and then went on. "From now on, the Moon again becomes gradually visible in the night sky. Beginning as a very thin crescent open to the left, it becomes brighter and brighter until it resembles a capital D. We say, the Moon is *waxing* and approaches the *first quarter*," and Sirius drew, in direction of his arrows, another circle with just the left half blackened that, during this phase, is not visible from Earth.

"Just after sunset, we see the *first quarter* of the Moon high up in the south. The right half of its face visible to us – just one quarter of the Moon's surface – is illuminated by the Sun."

"I know, I know, what comes next!" Staila jumped up driven by impatient excitement, took the pen from her friend's paw and started to draw a white circle to the left of the Earth. "When I see our Moon here, I see it completely round and bright."

"Very good!" Sirius and the Telescope praised the cat in unison, "it is *full Moon* and rises in the east when the Sun sets in the west."

The cat grinned and looked happily from one friend to the other.

Sirius went and took his pen back from Staila: "During the following nights the Moon's face begins to darken until it is once again just a thin crescent, but this time open to the right, like a capital C."

"Correct", agreed the Telescope, "at this time, the Moon is *waning*."

Sirius drew another circle on the paper, this time at the bottom, below the Earth, with the right half black as seen from Earth. "And this is how Staila would see the Moon about one week after full Moon - when its phase is called *last quarter*."

The Telescope hummed briefly in agreement: "Each of the phases of the *lunation – new Moon, first quarter, full Moon,* and *last quarter* lasts about one week. Together, they take up, as was said before, 29.5 days. For a long time, this was the basis for the duration of a month in the so called *lunar calendar*. It was later replaced by the *solar calendar* still used today, in which the length of the month is calculated from the duration of Earth's orbit around the Sun, which takes 365.25 days. One year has 12 months and so by dividing the number of days in a year by 12

we get the average length of a month – 30.4 days. Each day in the calendar has 24 hours which corresponds to one rotation of Earth around its axis. Therefore, to make everything work together and to avoid shifts in holiday dates and the beginnings of seasons caused by the four tenths of a day…"

"Which are 9.6 hours per month!" the cat interrupted the Telescope.

"Correct, Staila!" agreed their robotic friend in genuine admiration," so in order to avoid date shifts caused by these 'extra hours' people agreed to have months with some extra hours lasting 31 days followed by months with less hours lasting 30 days. And because not even this could solve the problem completely, people shortened February to 28 days, allowing 29 days just every 4 years. Such a year is then called a *leap year*."

The Telescope directed his tube to a dome wall area covered with all kind of images. "This is a photograph I made some time ago together with Václav here at Lü-Stailas. In fact, it's made of 5 pictures which were carefully registered in the computer. We see the Moon in its various phases above the mountains of the Val Müstair. The full Moon is right in the middle, above the Ortler, flanked on both sides by the first - right - and last - left - quarter. Framing the whole are on both sides the thin crescents just after and before new Moon."

Collage of Moon phases above the mount Ortler

"This is really an excellent collage", exclaimed Sirius. Not many are capable of honoring the good work of others like this. Suddenly, a thought crossed Staila's mind. "Is there a time when we actually can see the Moon during the day?"

"For sure. And the picture to show this hangs right there on the wall: the Moon during morning hours with Piz Daint!", assured the Telescope. "The Moon is still high up in the western sky while the Sun is already shining above the eastern horizon. By the way, the stars as well don't stop shining during the day. We just cannot see them in bright day light. Fortunately, the Moon appears much bigger to us than the stars, so we can still see it against the bright blue sky."

The Moon during the day above Piz Daint

CHAPTER 5:
WHEN DOES LUNA BLUSH

As Staila and Sirius still appeared full of interest and energy, the Telescope hummed and asked in a low voice: "Did either of you ever see a *Moon eclipse*?"

"Yes, sure. What a great event!", Sirius broke out in excitement. "Suddenly, the Moon's edge starts to darken and soon it looks as if a giant red hourglass passes in front of it."

Moon eclipse

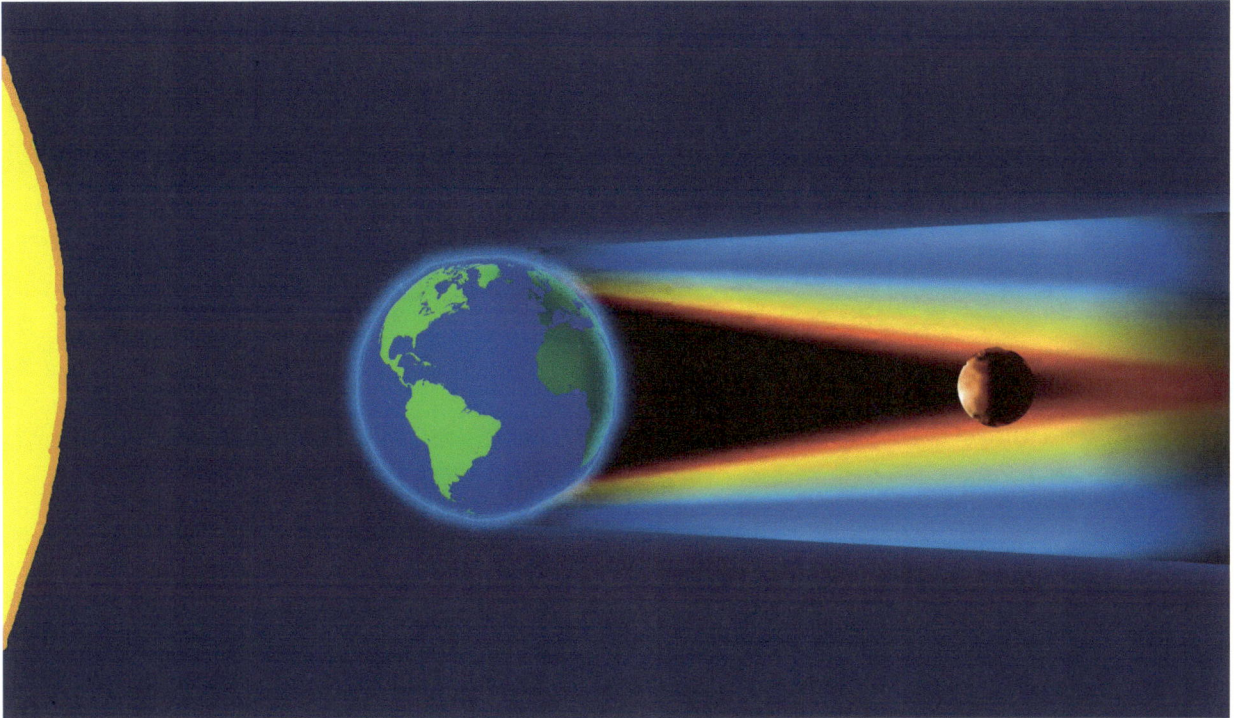

The 'blushing' Moon

"No, I have never seen this happen", said Staila sadly with a big sigh. She was a few years younger than her doggie friend.

The Telescope winked at her with his shiny eyepiece and tried to comfort her. "Now, now, you just have to be a little patient – the next eclipse will come for sure."

Sirius continued in his excitement: "This fantastic event happens when the Moon enters Earth's shadow. If you'd like, Staila, I can again draw this for you."

Immediately, Staila's curiosity made her stretch her neck to better see what he was drawing. And while Sirius was drawing, the Telescope explained: "A Moon eclipse occurs up to three times per year. But in most cases, just a small part of the Moon gets obscured and we barely notice it. It's called a *partial Moon eclipse*. Only when the Sun, the Earth, and the Moon are exactly aligned and cover each other perfectly, is it time for a *total Moon eclipse*. The last total eclipse ocurred in Europe on September 28, 2015 and lasted 72 minutes. The next one will take place on July 27, 2018 with a duration of 103 minutes!"

Sirius was almost done with his drawing. "I must emphasize that even during a total Moon eclipse, the Moon remains visible. However, it gets a mysterious, dark-red color. This happens because sunlight, when it passes Earth's atmosphere, is bent and scattered, so that the light falls obliquely on the eclipsed surface of the Moon…"

"Now, I am really starting to have a hard time understanding you, Sirius", Staila admitted in a somewhat confused way.

"Don't worry, another drawing will help", said Sirius in a reassuring voice. He not only likes to observe and explore the world around him but really loves to put its distinctive features and beauty on paper. "Rays of white sunlight can be bent, or refracted, when they pass different media. This makes them change direction and also breaks them up into single colors. A familiar example is the rainbow where light is refracted on the surface of raindrops. The same happens with sunlight entering Earth's atmosphere."

Sirius interrupted his explanations and peeked at Staila through his bushy eyebrows. Did she know what the atmosphere was?

"Don't look like that!", said the little cat sulkily, "of course, I know about the atmosphere. After all, I live at Lü-Stailas and have picked up all kinds of things from the astronomers' conversations… It's the thin gas envelope around Earth containing oxy-gen and water which are essential for life."

"Very good", laughed Sirius placidly and drew the Earth surrounded by a blue layer of atmosphere. "You see, the sunlight comes from here. By the way, in empty space one sees the light only when it shines straight into the eyes or when it hits an object."

"You mean, like the Earth or the Moon", Staila cut in.

"Yes, exactly. Sunlight, like a spotlight, illuminates planets and their moons and when it arrives on Earth, it penetrates and illuminates also the atmosphere."

"But then, how come we see the eclipsed Moon in red?" Staila returned to the original question.

"Naturally, because the sunlight not only illuminates the atmosphere but also gets bent in it and the individual rainbow colors are being scattered. Blue is scattered the most and red the least. Therefore, it is mainly the red portion of light that reaches the eclipsed Moon and turns it dark-red."

Evidently, the entire party was having a lot of fun and basked in the evening's balm. Outside, the Moon and stars were shining in the silence of the night and the air was permeated by the scent of grass and alpine flowers.

CHAPTER 6:
WHY CAN'T WE SWIM IN THE OCEANS ON THE MOON?

"My dear ones", began the Telescope, "in the meantime, I prepared for you a wonderful spectacle." Staila and Sirius stared at their knowledgeable friend and, with impatient curiosity, perked up their ears not to miss a word of what the Telescope was ready to share.

"But first another question: When you look at the Moon carefully just with the naked eye, you recognize bright and dark areas on its surface – the Man-In-The-Moon." The Telescope pondered its last words. "Why could that be?"

"Oh, well….I would say these are features of the Moon's landscape. The dark areas could be oceans and the brighter ones - dry land", said Staila hesitantly.

Sirius immediately attacked her suggestion: "But there is neither liquid water nor atmosphere on the Moon."

The Telescope, however, defended the cat: "Actually, you almost got it right, Starlet. The spots on the Moon remained a great secret for a long time. A lot of stories and legends about them were coursing arround. Finally, only exact observation and science demonstrated the lunar surface to be stony, covered with gravel, and formed by high mountains, seas and deep valleys. But the main features are craters everywhere! But Sirius is right as well – you would search in vain for water and air. Although some years ago astronomers successfully detected water crystals in Moon rocks and some indication of a very thin atmosphere, it is never enough to support life as we know it."

Staila was somewhat disappointed and her whiskers drooped. But a sudden turning of the Telescope and its beeping sounds made her quickly regain her inquisitive enchantment.

"And do you know who was the first to observe the Moon through a Telescope?", the robotic friend asked enthusiastically.

Since nobody responded, it continued: "Galileo Galilei, a scholar living close to Florence in the Italian province of Tuscany between the 16th and 17th century. For many years he observed the skies and drew, described and measured everything as precisely as possible. In his work he showed that the until then firmly established *geocentric*

Galileo Galilei

view of the cosmos, namely, that Earth is fixed in the center and Sun, planets and all the stars were turning around it, seemed wrong. Galileo's observations suggested the Earth to be a planet orbiting the Sun with all the other planets. With other European astronomers like Giordano Bruno, Niklaus Copernicus, Johannes Kepler, or Tycho de Brahe, Galileo started to teach the *heliocentric* view of the solar system and modern astronomy. This way astronomy became an exact science and began to detach itself from astrology, which claims to be able to foresee events and personality features from the positions of planets in the sky.

It lasted several centuries until society was ready for the radically new thoughts of these great scientists. Galileo himself, for his evidently uncomfortable and forbidden teaching, was sentenced by the Church to lifelong home prison in 1633."

Sirius growled disdainfully: "I read that Giordano Bruno was burned at the stake 33 years earlier because of his belief that our Sun is but one of an infinite number of stars."

"Moreover, Galileo had to revoke all his theories as being sick inventions", lamented the Telescope. "His only consolation remained in his sky observations. He remained charged with heresy for his entire life and his damaged reputation was whitewashed by the Pope only in 1992!"

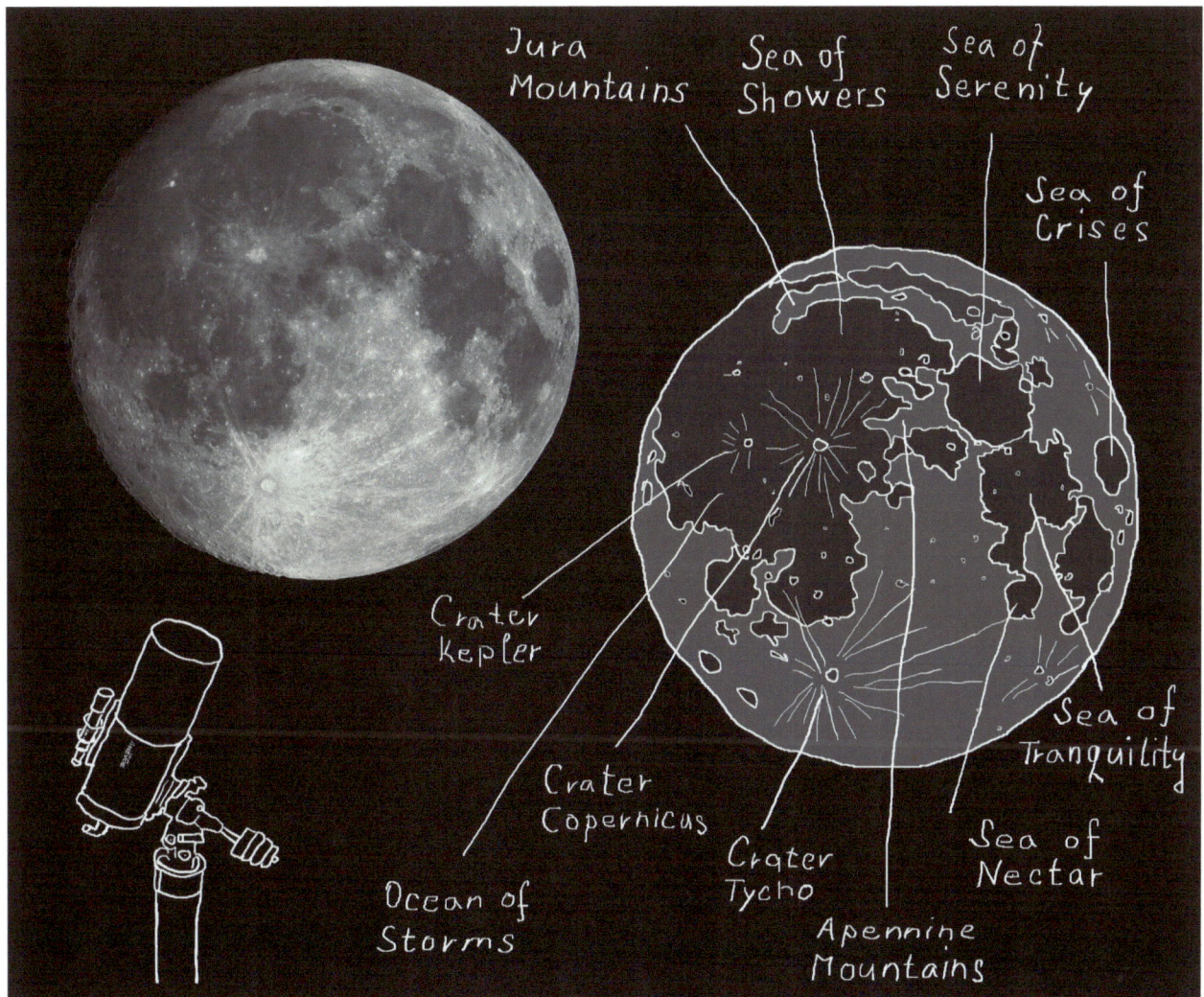

Observation of the Moon

Staila and Sirius looked at each other in disbelief. How could the correctness of the heliocentric science still be doubted in the 20th century with mankind already starting to conquer space?

But the Telescope continued: "With the help of modern technology we now have very precise maps of the Moon, including the half that is turned away from us. Space craft have been sent into orbit around the Moon in order to take photographs of its dark side as well."

Scientists have given very lovely names to the lunar landscapes: Sea of Tranquility, Sea of Serenity, or Ocean of Storms. There are also the Apennines and Jurassic Mountains, like in Italy and Switzerland."

There the Telescope exclaimed enthusiastically: "And now comes my promised show!" Sirius and Staila looked speechlessly as their friend gave computer commands for its automatic slewing to the Moon. Suddenly, its big tube started to turn in direction of the silvery disc floating high in the night sky. "Thanks to my robotic mount – my brain with all its gears and electronics is hopefully up and running correctly," the Telescope joked, "and also thanks to my motors I can move very precisely. Therefore, I can target any object in the sky and follow it for hours without losing it in the eyepiece. At the same time, I always stay connected to the computer."

When all was ready, the scope hummed with confidence and gave our friends a red sign. With one leap the cat and dog were at its side; they climbed the ready chair and one after the other looked through the eyepiece. "Wow! We have never seen the Moon so up close! How bright it is - like from a space ship!"

Immediately, Sirius took his pad, writing down and drawing all he just had heard and had recently seen: the Moon with its seas, oceans, mountains and innumerable craters.

"The entire surface is mountainous and covered by *regolith*."

"With what – relith?"

"No, *regolith* – a loose material consisting

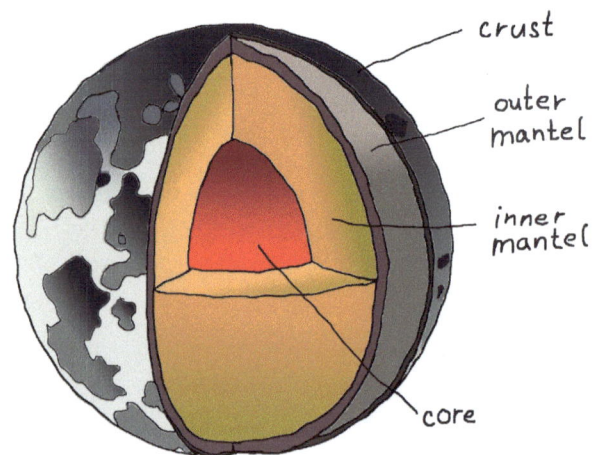

The interior of the Moon

of dust, soil, and broken rock of varying size", the Telescope corrected the cat and continued: "Strangely, the launched space probes found hardly any seas and big craters on the dark side, just some mid-sized and small ones." Sirius took his eye from the eyepiece: "But why is the lunar surface so rocky, stony, and dusty?"

"And where do all the craters come from?", joined in Staila.

"If you are really interested to know, I will tell you", started their robotic friend. His two companions became completely silent, not to miss one word of what was about to come.

"In a very distant past, more than four and a half billion years ago, the Moon was a giant glowing ball. When its surface started to cool, it hardened and formed the Moon crust. Something like the skin of custard while cooling… Beneath this crust, however, remained a partly liquid and hot mantle. Finally, at the Moon's center, there glows even today a metallic core like coal in a furnace. Initially, the young Moon was bombarded over millions of years with meteorites and asteroids. Their hits formed craters of various sizes in the Moon crust. Some were thousands of miles wide with walls as high as the Alps! Others, on the other hand, were so small you could hardly see them."

"Wait, please", interrupted Staila. "What are asteroids and meteorites?"

"An asteroid is a minor planet orbiting the Sun like a regular planet. There are millions of such asteroids and other small bodies in the solar system. They can crash into each other, combine, or destroy each other. Sometimes, they can throw each other off their orbits and leave the solar system or they can get in close proximity of a larger body and fall down on it."

"Yeah, that's similar to my game of marbles", Staila chuckled, comparing the collisions of heavenly bodies to her favorite game. "Either, the marbles push each other out of the way, or, if close enough to the hole, they roll into it following circular paths."

The Telescope grumbled in agreement. "Meteorites are much smaller than asteroids and there is also a multitude of them. Those still flying high up in the sky or orbiting a planet are correctly called meteoroids. They become meteorites only after they hit the ground."

The Telescope looked briefly in direction of its friends and saw that both were really taken by its words. "If a meteoroid gets too close to a planet or moon, the gravitational pull on it can get so strong that it plummets to the body's surface. At most times, it is completely shattered and forms a crater. Consequently, it damages the Moon's surface and older craters, so that broken rocks, gravel, and dust are formed – precisely the definition of regolith."

The Telescope checked quickly if the Moon was still centered in the eyepiece. "Thousands of meteorites carved one crater after the other into the lunar surface. The satellite was also heavily shaken by strong moonquakes, its crust broke open, and the newly formed craters became filled with lava from the Moon's interior. Fiery seas formed, cooking and blistering. But, finally, over millions of years, they cooled down and turned to dark and cold rock."

"Oh boy, well then, of course!", Staila laughed out, amused, "in such a rocky sea, nobody can really swim! No swimming, no skating. Nothing but rocks, dust, and dirt."

Asteroids and meteorites bombarding the young Moon

CHAPTER 7:
GODDESS THEIA AND THE BIRTH OF THE MOON

By now, the air outside was chilly. Sirius and Staila were happy to be inside the dome, protected from the cold of the mountain nights.

"But where does the Moon actually come from? Has it always been orbiting the Earth?", asked Sirius.

"Nobody knows for sure", the Telescope sighed, "and opinions still differ about its origin. Some time ago, astronomers thought the matter of the Moon had been torn from the Earth's crust by *centrifugal forces* and left the ocean floors as scars..."

"What is the centrifugal force?", asked Staila.

Sirius looked at her and replied: "This is an apparent force acting outwards on all bodies moving on a curved path. All loose objects fly away. It is like the game of statues. When I turn you around and suddenly let go – the centrifugal force will hurl you away from me."

"Oh come on – so now I am nothing but some sort of 'spinning body' ", said the cat, half sulking, half amused.

Their robotic friend continued its explanations: "Others think the Moon may have come from the depths of space and became trapped by Earth and forced into its orbit. But the most widely accepted theory among astronomers seems to be that the young Earth, just some 50 million years old and still glowing hot, collided with a Mars-sized body named Theia. In this giant impact, enormous amounts of melted material from Theia and from Earth were supposedly ejected into space and started to circle the Earth, forming our Moon. Theia got its beautiful name from the Greek goddess of light. According to the legend she is the mother of the Moon goddess Luna, the god of the Sun, Helios, and the goddess of dawn, Aurora. Her parents, on the other hand, are the god of the heavens, Uranus, and Gaia, the goddess of the Earth."

Sirius wagged his tail joyfully, since he absolutely loved the world of Greek legends. Already was he imagining the collision of two planets, the creation of the Moon, and amidst all of it a lovely goddess Theia.

Staila liked the picture, yet she wanted

to know more: "Well, now I know how the Moon came into existence and what its landscape looks like. But can one of you tell me what the size of the Moon is and how far it is from us? Is it cold there or hot?"

With his paw Sirius grabbed the book that he saw on the table next to the Telescope, opened it at the chapter about the Moon and started reading: "On average, the distance between Moon and the Earth is 384,400 kilometers. The Moon's orbit is almost circular and measures approximately 2.5 million kilometers. The diameter of the Moon is about 3,500 kilometers and its average surface temperature is minus 23 degrees Celsius."

"Oh my…so the Moon is pretty cold!", exclaimed Staila surprised. "We have had a chill like this on just a couple of days per year here in the Val Müstair."

"Yep, but just imagine", replied Sirius and continued reading, "the temperature on the Moon can drop to a nasty minus 240 degrees or it can soar to scorching 123 degrees - meaning, that without protection, we would either freeze rock-solid or we might get slowly roasted in the heat. It is also known that on the Moon everything is six times lighter than on Earth."

"Great! So I would weigh hardly one kilo, and so would you", said Staila and laughed at the thought.

Formation of the Moon and the goddess Theia

CHAPTER 8:
A MAGIC LIGHT BEAM AND THE BEGINNING OF THE EXPEDITION

Staila and Sirius again became absorbed by the Moon's image in the eyepiece. Suddenly, the kitty exclaimed wishfully: "Oh, how I'd love to fly there once!"

And Sirius added quickly: "Yes, it has always been my dream to become an astronaut".

"Would it really be your great wish to visit the Moon?", asked the Telescope. Then, he turned towards the two, blinked its eyepiece and whispered mysteriously: "Because if that's really what you want, I can make your wish come true…"

"Really? And HOW?", our four-legged friends shouted out as one, eager to start an adventure.

"I have magic powers and I can cast a spell on you. You will be able to travel through space, feeling neither hot nor cold, and one deep breath will provide you with enough air and force to last a whole space odyssey."

Staila and Sirius were stretched to breaking point in the expectation of the things to come. Suddenly, the Telescope turned with a gentle vibration to a metal pointer lying on its table. It had one end with a tiny lens and a button on its side.

"This is my starry pointer. It sends out a green light beam and can touch the stars."

Without hesitation, Staila grabbed the pointer and pushed the button. Wow – instantly, she touched the Moon with a long green shiny finger!

The Telescope continued to think aloud: "I guess, first, I should send you to the *Sea of Tranquility*. It is there, that man landed on the Moon for the first time. Staila, please, place the pointer on my tube so that it points exactly in the direction where I am looking. Fix it in that position with this Velcro tape in order to prevent it from falling down. And place the tape over the button so that the pointer keeps shining. It has to point exactly in direction of your landing place on the Moon."

Our little friends were trembling with impatience while they were holding their breath, with their hearts pounding crazily with excitement. Curiosity and spirit of adventure were stronger than fear.

The beginning of an expedition

The telescope blinked with its red and blue lights and declared solemnly in a low voice: "I hereby transfer part of my magic powers to you. They will protect you on your space travels and will enable you to fly on the magic light beam."

The two four-legged friends looked at each other with great enthusiasm.

"Oh yes, take this little walkie-talkie with you as well. We need to stay in touch all the time. And here you have another small magic pointer that will speed up your transfers on the Moon. You just need to point it where you want to go, push the light button, and then firmly hold onto the pointer with your paws. Sirius, better attach both immediately to your collar," advised the telescope knowing how important proper preparation is for such an expedition. He was almost dewy-lensed, like everybody parting from friends.

"Alright my dears, the time has come. Take care of yourselves and of the lunar landscape, and respect nature, of which the Moon, the whole cosmos, and we are all a part. And now, I wish you a successful and safe journey full of adventures and new inspirations!"

The Telescope aimed the magic beam precisely on the southern rim of the Sea of Tranquility and Sirius and Staila went closer to the green pointer light, with their paws ready to grasp it. They started the count-down they had heard so many times on TV: "Ten, nine, eight, seven, six, five, four, three, two, one, LIFTOFF," and their paws firmly closed around the magic light beam...

CHAPTER 9:

LUNA AND APOLLO

The green light gave a flash and before you could say "twenty-one", the magic beam pulled our friends up to the Moon. Suddenly, they were on the edge of a mid-sized hole in the ground filled with grey sand and fine gravel. Already their feet slipped and they both rolled over to the bottom. Without hurting themselves, they rolled softly and slowly.

"Woof," barked Sirius in surprise.

"Oh gosh," gasped Staila.

Both got up on their feet and brushed off their fur. Looking over the border of the hole they were in, they saw a vast plain without trees and blue sky. Above their heads began the bottomless, black space with thousands of stars.All around them were just cliffs, rocks, and many holes, large and small. Some were really very deep and wide so it would take many days to cross them – others were small and many even very tiny, like dimples on a car after a hail storm.

"These must be the famous lunar craters," whispered the cat into the dog's ear, although there was nobody around to be disturbed.

The friends crawled out of their crater and softly slid down along its outer wall. They had a strange feeling of levitation. Soon, they found out the best way to move – gentle swaying jumps on all fours. Suddenly, the walkie-talkie on Sirius' collar started to give off crackling sounds.

"Hello, …ello, do you ..ear me?" came the somewhat crackling voice of the Telescope, frequently breaking off.

"Yes, yes! We are fine", Staila responded readily. She was so happy to hear their friend's voice from Earth.

"Great! Big rel….ve for me as …ell. Do you see the …ast plain reaching out to the horizon? Should be right in front of y… . That is the Sea of Tr…quility. The Apollo 11 mission l…nded on its southe… shores on July 20, 1969, br…ging the first …umans to the Moon. The crew were the Amer…can astronauts Michael Collins, Neil Armstrong, and Edwin 'Buzz' Aldrin."

Sirius and Staila carefully scrutinized the surroundings.

"While astronaut Mike …ollins stayed in orbit aboard the C…mmand Module Columbia (named after Christopher Columbus who discovered America in the 15th century), the two others boarded the Lunar Module Eagle (the symbol of the USA), sepa…ted from Columbia, and descended to the Moon's …rface. After landing, Armstrong conf…med the success with the famous …ords 'The Eagle has landed'."

At this moment, Sirius jumped a little forward, bent his head and started sniffing: "Come quick, Staila! I found tracks of large boots. They could lead us to the exact landing site."

While the cat tried to get to her friend with a couple of wavy jumps, he was already following the tracks, head down like a real hunting dog. Suddenly, Staila stopped and her whiskers curled in excitement.

"There – I see something like a small harvester with funny big mirrors. And next to it a box with antennas!"

The crackling voice from the walkie-talkie on Sirius' collar came again: "Think, this …ould be some sort of scien…fic instruments, left-overs from the Apollo …ission. The landing site was called *Tranquility Base*."

As quickly as the reduced gravity on the Moon allowed them, Sirius and Staila reached the abandoned instruments and examined them carefully. On the ground were many tracks from crenate boots - imprints left for ever in the deep sand. Here, neither wind nor rain could blow or wash them away.

Tranquility Base

Sirius, true to his canine nature, quickly marked several bigger stones so he and Staila wouldn't get lost. Suddenly, he stopped and barked exuberantly. He had found something interesting.

"Do you see this metal frame and the legs? I guess this must be the lower portion from the Lunar Module Eagle left over during the liftoff of its ascent stage.

This way the astronauts saved some weight while getting back to Columbia. After reaching the Command Module, they jettisoned the ascent stage back to the Moon and returned safely to Earth."

And because Sirius has a vivid imagination, he immediately imagined the Modules Eagle and Columbia at Tranquility Base and in orbit around the Moon.

"Hey, look, there at the horizon – that's surely the American flag. That's very reassuring. So it is true!"

"What do you mean?" asked Staila surprised.

"Because I heard there are actually people who do not believe that humans really did land on the Moon! They say it's all nonsense. So they argue the American flag could not be seen billowing since there is no air and wind on the Moon. Now we know that the flag is held horizontally by a thin rod… ."

The Telescope's squeaking voice came again from the radio: "Many people want to just appear …teresting but don't …ave enough brains to think before speaking."

"I see clouds coming on the horizon!" miaowed Staila in disbelief. "But didn't you say, there is no atmosphere on the Moon?"

"There won't be any rai… from …ese clouds. It's a storm of very fine and sharp dust carried by tiny elec…ical particles having the same charge as the …oon's surface."

"It's like with same-pole magnets – the more you try to approach them, the stronger they repel each other," Sirius entered the conversation.

"Oh yes, I know that very well. I have a magnetic mouse that I can chase with a magnetic rod," Staila immediately remembered one of her favorite toys.

"For the ast..nauts and their inst…ments, the Moon dust represents a …eat danger. It sticks to everythi… as if it was wet. But there are not even traces of …ater. The dust particles enter every…ere, even the …allest crannies. They even get into space suits and can …arm the astronaut's skin and lungs. A big threat is also seizing up and damage to machines and s…tific devices. Up till now, there is just no way how to prote… space crews efficiently from this dust."

Meanwhile, the dust clouds had, fortunately, changed direction and did not represent a threat anymore. A big relief for our friends.

But as if this was not enough, suddenly, Sirius made a jump: "Careful, Staila!" A small meteorite zipped close by his head and landed in the sand.

Already, the Telescope warned in a worried voice: "Got a visit from a met…rite, correct? You are p…tected by my spell but still you have to be …ery careful. there is a …stant rain of meteorites on the Moon, although much weaker than many millions years a… . Since there is no lunar atmosph…, unfortunately, these things don't burn up above ground. So don't expect to see them there as ...ooting stars or meteors.

Worried, Sirius and Staila looked quickly up to check for possible danger. This time, however, there was nothing but the black silence of the deep cosmos.

Sirius and Staila looking towards their planet Earth

CHAPTER 10:
MOON BUGGY AND THE FALLEN ASTRONAUT

"Would you like to know a great wish of mine?" asked Sirius. "To drive once in my life one of the three lunar vehicles left on the Moon by the astronauts."

"But to do this you are in the ...rong place. You ...ave to move on. The reason is, there were ...tually dozens of expeditions explor... the Moon. The first ones were without crews. They were space probes that ...amined and photo...phed the Moon from orbit or after landing on it."

"Still, the most fantastic were those which brought humans to our satellite," marveled Sirius.

"Oh yes, of course. But before someone ...ould finally take a buggy ride on the Moon, there preceded endless efforts of mankind to explore the ...orld and nature's laws. When Neil Armstrong touched as the first human being the lunar surfa... he solemnly proclaimed: 'One small step for a man, one giant leap for mankind.' Sadly, Neil left us on August 25, 2012 at the age of 82 in the Ame...can State of Ohio."

Sirius and Staila became silent and looked in awe at the boot tracks left here for many years by Neil and Buzz.

The Telescope continued: "All ...veloped industrial countries ...articipated in space ex...oration. But the prime role in the quest for the cosmos and in the flight ...ograms to the Moon must be attributed to mainly two world powers: the USA and the Soviet Union. Both gave their probes and space flight ...issions beautiful names of mighty and famous gods from anti... tales. The Soviets called them after the Greek ...oddess of the Moon, *Luna*, and the Ameri....s named their lunar flight missions ...ter *Apollo*, the Greek god of pilgrim... settling new worlds, an excellent archer, and the master of all Muses."

While the Telescope was explaining, Sirius and Staila jumped up and down and levitated across Tranquility Base and continued to check out the mission remains. They found a pair of boots from a space suit, a camera that Neil left behind, and a few garbage bags.

"Who was succe...ful first between both ...untries was often just a matter of a few weeks. The first ...hicle on the Moon was a robot launched by the Soviet rocket Luna 17 in 1970 and landed on the weste... shores of the Sea of Showers. Its name was *Lunochod* meaning *Walking on the Moon* in Russian. The vehicle was ...trolled from

Earth and ran on solar ...atteries for almost a year. During that ti..., it drove over 10 thousand meters examin... and photographing the lunar surface. When you get back to Earth, I will show you a ...icture of the Moon with all the im...tant Luna and Apollo missions indicated."

"But, surely, the only thing you would like to know about now, is where to find the closest lunar vehicle in which the astronauts were driving around, isn't it, Sirius?" the Telescope asked the dog with an understanding voice.

"Woof, woof," agreed Sirius and jumped up in joy so that it took quite a while before he came back down again on all fours.

"In 1971, the crew of the Apollo 15 ...ission was the first to take a lun.. vehicle with them and called it the Lunar

Luna and Apollo

Expeditions to the Moon

Rover. Soon, however, it was affectionately called Moon Buggy, like the …mous off-road …creational …hicle. That name then stuck for good."

Sirius was so absorbed with listening he forgot to look where he was going. Before he could react, he stumbled over a rock and was making one flip after another. After Staila was sure nothing happened to her friend, she started laughing: "You were popping up and down like the balloon we use to throw around in the garden."

But Sirius just brushed off the dust impatiently. "Shhh! Don't disturb."

"The Moon Buggy could reach a …eed of up to 12 km/h and allowed the crew to explo… a much larger area away from the …unar Module than had been po...

ble just by jumping around on …issions without it. Ho…ver, to drive the Buggy on the Moon is far from easy! Everywhere it went, it left a huge cloud of dust behi…, jumped over stones and rocks back and forth like a wild pony and had …ard time to keep from turning over."

"But WHERE exactly can we find the Moon Buggy?" Sirius asked with great excitement.

Suddenly, the walkie-talkie went silent except for some static noise. It didn't take long and the sudden silence started to evoke a strange feeling of loneliness…Sirius and Staila feared they may have lost connection with Earth. Fortunately, after a short while, which seemed like eternity, the voice of their friend came back.

"OK, here I …ave it. Sorry, friends, but, I had to dig out the exact coor…nates to show you the right direc…n to move. Look at the horizon. A green sign from my magic …ointer will show you in which direc…n you have to point the one I gave you befo… you left and which Sirius attached to his collar. Like this, I can guide you to the Apennine …untains, to the landing site of

Sirius and Staila did exactly as told. As soon as they saw the sign on the horizon, they grabbed each other's paw, aimed their pointer in that direction and

pushed the button. Instantly, they found themselves hundreds of kilometers away from where they just had been, amidst the mountainous landscape of the lunar Apennine region. They couldn't believe their eyes. Right in front of them, on a close-by hill, there it was in all its glory – the Moon Buggy! As much as the low gravity of the Moon allowed them, they started to stumble and jump as hard as they could to get to the rover. Impatiently, Staila suddenly made a big leap from a stone and, hop, landed right on the striped seat of the Buggy. That, however, was enough for the shaky vehicle to start rocking back and forth and moving down the hill. While gaining speed, it started to stir up a big cloud of dust.

"Heeeeelp!"

Sirius followed Staila as fast as he could. Full of fear, the poor little cat had crouched down and was now holding firmly onto the seat with all her claws. She waited for the inevitable crash on one of the big rocks nearby. However, the Moon Buggy didn't make it too far. Soon, its front wheels buried themselves deep into the sand and the rover came to a sudden stop. That, however, hurled Staila high up from the seat and she landed a couple of meters in front of the Buggy and remained there, motionless. Finally, Sirius arrived at the site and, full of fear and concern, started to hop around his friend, sniffing, and poking her gently with his nose. But as we all know, cats have nine lives and crashing on the Moon is by far not as damaging and painful as on Earth. So, after a while, Staila opened her eyes, lifted her tail above her head and got up on her feet.

"You are really very lucky, Staila," Sirius told his friend with a sign of rebuke in his voice.

When he saw his friend unharmed he turned to examine the Moon Buggy whether it may have received some damage. Since he found nothing significant, both friends gave a sigh of relief. That was a big load off their minds.

"That's it – no more Buggy riding," Sirius murmured for himself.

To be on the safe side, the doggie put a few rocks in front of the Buggy's wheels to prevent it from moving again and looked around. Not far from them, they remarked only now part of a metal plate sticking out from the sand. In front of it, between the familiar tracks of astronauts, lay a small silvery statue.

"We found a metal statuette and a plate with some names," they reported down to Earth.

The Telescope responded with a solemn voice: "That is a memorial to the cosmonauts and astronauts who at that time were known to have died in the furtherance of space exploration. The plaque shows fourteen names and in front of it is an aluminum sculpture called *Fallen Astronaut*."

Sirius and Staila looked down in silence. They always felt a strong humbleness and an almost sacred awe in front of those who gave their lives in the quest of knowledge.

Moon Buggy and the *Fallen Astronaut*

CHAPTER 11:
HOMESICK FOR THE VAL MÜSTAIR

From all the past adventures they went through in the last few hours, both friends suddenly felt very tired. Their eyes turned towards the dark above them and they saw, far-far away, their blue home planet Earth hovering in the sky. Instantly, they longed for nature flooded with warm sunlight, for the whispering of the wind, the bubbling flow of mountain streams, and the melodies of bird songs. They remembered the sounds of cow and sheep bells

Looking after friends

and the fragrance of cut grass in the meadows of the Val Müstair. They moved close to a group of craters and sat down in the dust.

Staila whispered: "Sirius, I am so exhausted and I feel so very homesick...." Her little voice broke and she stopped talking so that Sirius couldn't hear her sobbing. Slowly, she crawled into a small crater not far away and, sad as she was, put her forehead against its rim.

The lunar silence was suddenly cut by the soothing voice of their friend on Earth: "Now, now, my dears. You saw so many things and had so many adventures today – you learned so much. The path to knowledge is usually long and often painful. But you sure are no wimps. Since you already got so far, it would be a great shame not to finish your mission. And be assured - other new adventures are awaiting you!"

To Sirius, the voice of their friend gave new strength and confidence. "I must admit that I am a bit worn out. In a state like this, one sees everything in black. Alright then, Starlet, let's get a healthy nap. That will give us new strength and energy to continue our journey."

Staila's eyes were already closed and, to give a sign of agreement, she just, half asleep, briefly flicked her ears. After all, she still is one of the most inquisitive cats in the whole world – or at least in the Val Müstair. Sirius lay down at the base of the crater from which there already came the softly snoring and breathing sounds of his friend. He put his head on his forepaws and quicker than you can say Jack Robinson, he fell deeply asleep as well.

Far away on Earth, the Telescope heard the muffled whistling noises of his two friends soundly asleep. He turned off the radio so it couldn't startle them accidentally. He looked forward to all the other adventures that awaited them.

Gathering new forces for the journey

ABOUT THE AUTHORS

Jitka and Václav Ourednik – both university professors and researchers in the field of development and regeneration of the brain – worked at leading universities worldwide, including Harvard University in Boston MA (USA), University of Lausanne (Switzerland), Dalhousie University in Halifax NS (Canada), the Swiss Federal Institute of Technology in Zurich (ETHZ, Switzerland), Iowa State University in Ames IA (USA), and at the Czech Academy of Sciences in Prague (Czech Republic). Their work was published in journals such as Science, Nature and PNAS (Proceedings of the National Academy of Sciences, USA). They participated in the organization of international meetings and were invited to chair plenary sessions during scientific meetings and to give plenary and opening lectures.

In Jitka's and Václav's laboratories, both undergraduate and graduate students went through their training and they collaborated with experts at world-leading institutions like the MIT (Massachusetts Institute of Technology in Cambridge MA; USA), Yale University (New Haven CT, USA), the Karolinska Institutet in Stockholm (Sweden) and also with colleagues from the Czech Academy of Sciences in Prague.

During their scientific career, both received several honors and prizes. Among them are: Invitation to give the Nobel Forum Lecture during the Nobel Forum for Junior Faculty at the Karolinska Institutet in Stockholm (Sweden, 2003), First Prize offered by the Parkinson's Action Network and the Michael J. Fox Foundation for development of new methodologies in tracing of neural stem cells (USA, 2000), and a Pfizer Prize in Neuroscience for the co-authorship in a study of the genetic bases of brain development published in Science (1998).

Outside of their research in neuroscience, Jitka and Václav have always been fond of stargazing, astro- and nature photography, as well as writing popular science articles and books for young readers. For these reasons, and after over 30 years of a successful research career, they decided to realize their dream and create an astrophotography center in Europe.

At the beginning of 2008, they returned to Switzerland and, after a long and careful search for the ideal place, discovered the tiny village of Lü high up in the eastern Swiss Alps in the canton Graubünden. Their genuine enthusiasm was infectious and within two years, with the support of the authorities from county and canton, the *Alpine Astrovillage Lü-Stailas* was inaugurated in December 2009, during the International Year of Astronomy. In the local Romansh language, Lü-Stailas means *Light of Stars*.

The prime goal of the Center is to inspire the interested – beginner or advanced – to observe and photograph the cosmos under excellent conditions. The founders also strive to raise public awareness of the need to protect natural habitats from human sprawl, which results in the ever-expanding light pollution.

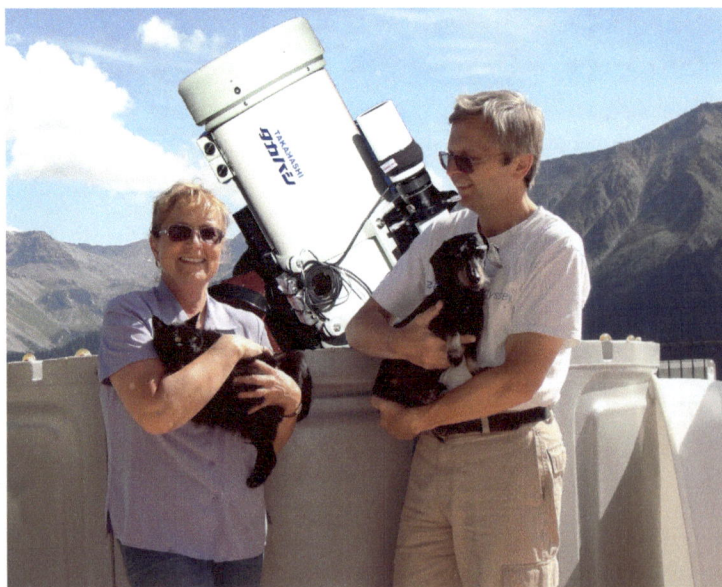

Jitka and Václav with three friends